HOW TO BE A SILVER SURFER

A beginner's guide to the internet

Second edition

Emma Aldridge

BOOKS

Published by Age Concern England
1268 London Road
London SW16 4ER

First published 2001
Reprinted 2001, 2002
This edition 2003

Editor Ro Lyon
Production Vinnette Marshall
Design and typesetting GreenGate Publishing Services, Tonbridge, Kent
Printed in Great Britain by Bell & Bain Ltd, Glasgow

A catalogue record for this book is available from the British Library.
ISBN 0-86242-379-1

Whilst the advice and information contained in this book is believed to be true and accurate at the time of going to press, neither Age Concern England nor the author can accept any legal responsibility or liability for any errors or omissions that may be made. Please note that while the agencies or products mentioned in this book are known to Age Concern, inclusion here does not constitute a recommendation by Age Concern for any particular product, agency or service.

Every effort has been made to trace copyright holders in all copyright material in this book. The editor regrets if there has been any oversight and suggests that the publisher is contacted in any such event.

Bulk orders
Age Concern England is pleased to offer customised editions of all its titles to UK companies, institutions, or other organisations wishing to make a bulk purchase.
For further information, please contact the Publishing Department at the address on this page. Tel: 020 8765 7200. Fax: 020 8765 7211. Email: books@ace.org.uk

Contents

About the author

Emma Aldridge is the National Development Manager for IT and Older People for Age Concern England (www.ageconcern.org.uk) and represents Age Concern on issues relating to technology and older people.

Acknowledgements

I have developed this book from a booklet and CD-ROM, called *Grasp the Nettle: A beginner's guide to the Internet*, also published by Age Concern.

Unless specified otherwise, the screen examples shown in this book have been generated using Internet Explorer 6 on a PC. The descriptions in the book apply to Internet Explorer 5 and above, and Netscape 4 and above, running on a PC.

Every effort has been made to ensure that the content is accurate at the time of writing.

My thanks to all the companies and other organisations for their permission to reproduce screen images taken from their Web sites.

My thanks to Mum, Dad and Sandie for putting these chapters to the test, and to Gideon.

Emma Aldridge

Chapter **1**

Introduction

Are you one of the many people who when you hear the words 'Web', 'Net' or 'surfing' still think of spiders, fishing and beaches? Do you go blank when a television or radio programme gives out an email address or do you wonder at this new language that seems to consist of lots of 'dots', 'ats' and 'coms'?

If you'd like to learn more about the Internet and this fantastic way of communicating, and obtaining and sharing information, then this book is for you. Although it will assume that you are not using a computer for the very first time, it will still attempt to break through the technical hype and take you on a step-by-step voyage of discovery. It will guide you through what you need to know to: use the World Wide Web; send and receive emails; go shopping and chat to people on the Internet. It will also introduce you to some of the ways in which the Internet can help you research your family history.

All the words that you see in ***bold italics*** are described in the glossary at the end of the book, and many of the Web sites mentioned are accompanied by screen images of the sites themselves. A more detailed list of some useful Web sites appears in the Appendix.

Chapter 2

What is the Internet?

The word 'Internet' is now used so freely in conversation, in news stories and in adverts, for example, that it can be a bit bewildering if you do not understand what it all means. In addition there are so many terms which are used interchangeably to describe very similar ideas ('Web', 'World Wide Web', 'Net', 'Cyberspace', 'Information Superhighway') that it is no wonder many of us feel confused by the whole thing.

Let's start at the beginning, and since we are talking about communication and information that means starting with a computer.

Some computers are simply stand alone pieces of equipment. They work in isolation, getting on with the jobs that are required of them but they do not meet or talk to anyone else.

Other computers are more sociable. They are connected to each other, and, like members of a large community, they can share things with each other. This sort of computer community is called a *network*.

The *Internet* is simply a global network of computers all connected to each other through telephone lines. When you use one of these computers to access the Internet you are *'online'*.

Other types of equipment can also be connected in order to share information and communicate with each other, such as digital television sets and mobile telephones. In this book, however, we concentrate on how you can use a computer to get started on the Internet.

Getting and sharing information

Every computer connected to the Internet is owned or used by people and organisations with information and expertise to share on just about any topic you can imagine. Being a member of the Internet 'club' is therefore like being a member of an enormous global library. The Internet equivalent to shelves crammed with millions of books and journals is the *World Wide Web (WWW)* or the *Web* for short.

Instead of reading the pages of a book, you simply look at the relevant pages of a *Web site* (sometimes referred to as 'surfing the Web'). It can also be a lot more exciting because you don't just have words, but can look at pictures and moving images, sometimes accompanied by sound, and you normally get the chance to communicate with the 'authors' of the Web site.

Communicating

Something else you can do when you get access to the Internet is send a message almost instantaneously to friends, family and other people all over the world. You do this by using *email*, short for electronic mail, which is the Internet's version of the postal service. Instead of putting a letter into the postbox and having to wait days for it to be picked up, delivered and a reply to arrive, you simply type a message on the computer keyboard, address it using an email address, and at the press of a key on your keyboard send it immediately to another computer anywhere in the world.

Meeting people

The most popular aspect of the Internet is that it is interactive. Not only can you find information about anything and everything at any time of the day, but you can also chat to other people looking for the same sort of things.

Email is a great way to swap messages with a person or a chosen group of people, but you can also use the Internet to share opinions and ideas with groups of new people all at once, by joining a *message board*, *chat site*, *newsgroup* or *mailing list*.

What else?

If that's not enough for you, the Internet can also provide you with new ways to:

- play your favourite card game or board game, against opponents who may be sitting at their computers on the other side of the world;
- research and book holidays, travel and other leisure time activities;
- read the latest news from any part of the world; and
- shop for books, food, presents and clothing.

Once you have access to the Internet, the whole world is at your fingertips.

Chapter 3

What do I need to access the Internet?

The essential bit of kit for getting access to the Internet is, of course, a computer. However, it is tricky knowing what kind of memory your computer is going to need, what *software* to run on it and what extras you need to get up and running on the Internet.

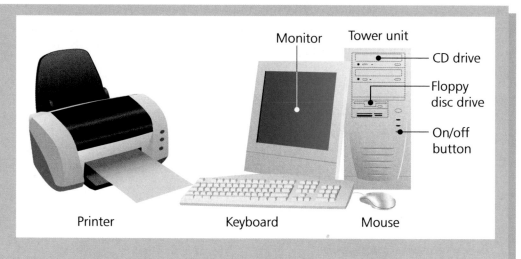

Monitor   Tower unit

CD drive

Floppy disc drive

On/off button

Printer   Keyboard   Mouse

Fig 1 – A computer system

1 The computer

Monitor
This is the 'TV screen' that displays the computer output.

Base unit or tower
Computers will have either a base unit or tower (never both). This is where the 'brains' of the computer are housed. A base unit is horizontal (so typically the monitor can rest on top), whereas a tower is upright (and so can fit by the side of the monitor or even out of sight below the desk).

The main features are usually the same: floppy disk drive, on/off button, reset button, CD or DVD drive and hard disk drive (which is hidden inside the box itself). These features are described in more detail in the next section 'Choosing the right computer'.

Mouse

This is connected to the base unit or tower and controls where letters, numbers and other characters typed into your keyboard appear on the screen. The mouse is also used to send instructions to your computer, to control operations such as starting up new software.

Keyboard

The keyboard is also connected to the base unit or tower. It consists of many lettered and numbered keys, and punctuation characters – just like a typewriter. It also contains keys like the tab key and arrow keys which can be used instead of your mouse to move around the screen, and the Return key (also called the Enter key) which you will often use to send a command to your computer.

Printer

Printers connect to computers and produce paper copies of what is displayed on the monitor.

A computer can also be called a Personal Computer, which you will often see and hear abbreviated as 'PC'.

Choosing the right computer

Your first choice is to consider whether you would prefer a laptop computer (laptop computers can also be called 'notebooks') or a desktop computer.

A laptop computer has the advantage that you can move it around, and use it at the kitchen table for example. Because they are smaller than desktop computers, they also take up less space. The disadvantages of laptop computers are that they are more expensive than desktop computers, the keyboards are smaller and so can be more difficult to use, and the screen size is smaller and so it can be more difficult to see the display.

Fig 2 – A laptop and a desktop computer

Your next choice should be the amount of money you are prepared to spend. If you have a budget of less than £500, then you will have enough for a second-hand computer and printer. A budget of between £500 and £1,000 will allow you to stretch to a new computer.

You do not necessarily need to have the latest computer to be able to use the Internet, but this still leaves a wide range of options and prices to consider.

Some of the options on offer include:

Drive
A device for reading and writing information to disk. These disks can be 'hard disks', 'floppy disks', 'compact disks' or 'DVD disks'.

Hard disk
The disk inside your computer where software programs and data are stored.

Disk capacity is measured in Megabytes (Mb), or Gigabytes (Gb) which are larger than Megabytes. Second-hand computers may start with hard disk capacity as low as 480Mb, meaning that they will hold a lot less information and fewer software programs than a newer computer with a hard disk capacity of 50Gb for example.

Floppy disk
Floppy disks are also used to store data but they can be removed and taken out of the computer. This means that they are ideal if you want to save some of your work and transfer it to another computer.

Fig 3 – Floppy disks and compact disks

Compact disk (CD)
Computer CDs are identical in appearance to a music CD. They can hold 656Mb of data (equivalent to approximately 500 floppy disks).

A CD that can only be read from is called a CD-ROM (which stands for 'Read Only Memory') and a CD which can be saved to is called a RW-CD (which stands for 'Read Write').

It is an advantage to choose a computer which includes a CD drive because it will allow you to load new software programs very easily.

Digital Versatile Disk (DVD)
A DVD holds over 20 times as much information as a CD.

Choose a computer with a DVD drive if you want to be able to watch films or play games on your computer.

Processor
This is one of the key factors in determining how quickly your computer will work. The faster the processor's speed (measured in MHz, which stands for MegaHertz) the more calculations and data the computer can process.

A computer with a 366MHz processor is sufficient for the Internet. But if you are intending to work with lots of graphics, sounds or video clips, it is advisable to look at a computer with around 700MHz. A 500MHz machine is fine if you want to play the odd computer game or scan and edit a few photographs.

RAM (Random Access Memory)

This is a series of small electrical circuit boxes, approximately 1cm square, held on 'cards' that slot inside the computer's base unit or tower. They temporarily store and access information on the computer.

Do not choose a computer which offers anything less than 64Mb, but if you can afford it, it is well worth trying to find a computer with at least 128Mb (just as for disks, Mb stands for 'Megabytes' and measures capacity or memory space).

Soundcard

Soundcards are needed in conjunction with external speakers to be able to hear audio (music, voice, etc) from your computer. A '16-bit' soundcard will be fine.

Monitor

Larger screens (advertised as 17 or 19 inch screens) are easier on the eye than smaller screens, but a small supplement (probably between £40 and £80) may be added to the price of the computer.

Software

New computers are often sold with what is called software included in the price. These are the computer programs which allow you to instruct your computer to browse the Web, send emails, type letters, help you manage your finances, etc.

Many computers will be supplied with software called *Microsoft Works* or *Microsoft Office* which allow you to do these common tasks.

If you are looking to buy a computer it is worth getting a computer which includes virus-checking software. This helps protect computers from dangerous files which move between computers over the Internet.

Printer

Colour inkjet printers currently cost between £50 and £80 and are ideally suited for home use. They can print photographs and pictures as well.

Scanner

A scanner can be bought as an optional piece of hardware. It converts paper documents into electronic files that can be kept on your computer. A very useful way of using a scanner is to scan photographs or maps and then email them to friends and family. Prices currently begin at about £65.

Licences and documentation

The computer hardware and the pre-installed software should come with a licence or certificate to prove legal ownership. This is particularly important if you choose to buy a second-hand computer. Before you buy a computer you should also find out whether you will receive instruction guides or user manuals.

Warranty and after-sales support

Ideally you should choose a computer which comes with a warranty of at least one year. If you do not want to rely solely on friends or family to help you with any problems you may have with your computer, then it is advisable to shop around for a good-value support service.

2 The modem

A *modem* can either fit inside your computer (and is called an *internal* modem) or is a little box which sits next to your computer and is linked via a cable to your computer (an *external* modem). It allows your computer to communicate with other computers over a standard telephone line. It converts the digital data from your computer into sound signals which are transmitted over the telephone line, and converts sound signals received by your computer back again into digital data which can be understood by your computer.

Modem speeds

If you are buying a modem you might see descriptions such as '56 Kbps' or '56K' used to describe modems for sale, but what does this mean?

The speed of a modem is measured in kilobits per second (Kbps). 56 Kbps is the speed limit – no modem can transfer information such as Web pages and email messages faster than this to and from your computer over a standard telephone line. Although slower modems may be slightly less expensive than faster models, the slower modems will add more to your telephone bill because they will take longer to transfer information.

Another tip is to look out for modems which are 'V.90' 56 Kbps modems. This is a standard and means that the modem will be able to talk to all other modems, whatever the make.

All new computers will come with an internal modem. Not all second-hand computers are supplied with modems, so you may need to buy one separately from a local computer store, by mail order or through a computer magazine for approximately £50. Internal modems are more complicated to install, so you may need to pay extra for a technician to do this for you.

3 The telephone line

Your computer and modem connect to other computers on the Internet via your telephone line. Sounds simple, doesn't it? Well it is … but a little planning will help you avoid some possible pitfalls.

You can use your existing telephone line for Internet use, but you will need a way to switch between your modem and your voice telephone. One way to do this is to scramble under your table every time you need to plug your modem cable into the telephone socket. Alternatively for a couple of pounds you can buy a simple accessory called a socket doubler from electrical retailers – it allows you to keep both your modem and your telephone connected to the telephone socket at the same time.

You can install a telephone extension, which means that you will be able to avoid having cables like spaghetti all over the place if your computer sits a distance away from your telephone socket.

The disadvantage of sharing a single telephone line between modem and telephone, is that you cannot make or receive telephone (voice) calls while connected to the Internet. If you access the Internet a lot, this might get a bit frustrating for friends and family who might still prefer to talk to you by telephone once in a while. It also presents a problem if you need to call an internet helpline because you won't be able to talk and be online (to describe the problem you're having) at once.

To avoid these little nuisances you could install an additional telephone line. Your telephone company will give you a new telephone number for the line, and you will be able to choose the room in which you want the socket installed. However, this will add to the cost. The price of an additional telephone line varies between different telephone companies, but expect to pay around £50 for the connection and around £10 each month for the rental.

If you have cable television or cable telephone, or live in an area where cable services are available, then you may be able to get a fast internet connection by cable. The monthly charge for this service may work out to be more expensive than the rental of a standard telephone line, and in a few cases you have to purchase a special cable modem, but the monthly charge may cover all your internet access as well, no matter how long you spend online.

The need for speed

Modem access via a standard telephone line is by far the most popular and cheapest way of connecting to the Internet from your home. However, sending information in this way can be very slow and can add pounds to your phone bill. If you are attracted by the idea of sending and receiving large amounts of information over the Internet, such as photographs and video broadcasts, then it is worth considering the cost of upgrading your telephone line to give you faster speeds.

Almost all telephone and cable operators now offer high-speed internet access called **broadband**, which has the additional advantages that it is 'always on', meaning that you pay a single monthly charge regardless of how much you use it, and it allows you to use the same line to make and receive calls while you are online. You will need to check first, however, that you live in an area which can access broadband, as it is still not available in many areas (particularly rural regions).

4 The Internet Service Provider

You will need to choose an **Internet Service Provider (ISP)** which provides you with the means to send and receive information over the telephone line to and from your computer.

Think of them as being like a telephone exchange. Your modem dials a special telephone number given by the ISP which calls one of the ISP's modems. This connects you to the rest of the Internet for the time that you are connected to your ISP.

Examples of ISPs include *Freeserve*, *AOL*, *Tiscali* and *ntlworld*. The main options offered by most ISPs are:

● **Pay-as-you-go** You will be charged according to the amount of time you spend on the Internet at the rate of making a local telephone call – so half an hour's connection on a BT line could cost you about 30 pence off-peak or £1.18 peak. If you think you will only use the Internet for email and occasional Web use, say a few hours a month, then this will probably be your best option.

- **Unmetered access** You will be charged a fixed monthly fee for unlimited use. This costs approximately £15, although you can sometimes get offers for a reduced price for the first three months. Read the terms and conditions carefully. Almost all require a BT line, and some ISPs impose restrictions, such as cut-off times to prevent continuous use, or compulsory minimum usage.
- **Off-peak deals** A combination of the last two; for example, a reduced monthly fee for unlimited internet use in the evening and at weekends (approximately £10), but charged at local telephone call rates during weekdays.
- **Broadband** As described in the previous section in this chapter, broadband gives you always-on, unmetered access up to ten times the speed of a standard modem. Expect to pay around £25 per month and an initial installation charge of around £100.

You can pick up CDs which allow you to sign up with an ISP at many retail outlets or attached to the pages of many computer magazines. You should simply be able to put the CD in the drive on your computer and follow the instructions given to you on the screen. Sometimes the ISP software is included with your computer if you buy it new; for example, computers bought from *PC World* stores are often set up to run *Freeserve*.

Other tips for choosing an ISP

Shopping around for an ISP can be a complicated business. Just like getting a good haircut, getting it right can save you a lot of hair-pulling at a later stage. Here are some of the things to look out for when choosing an ISP:

'How reliable is the ISP going to be?'

This is difficult to determine. The major ISPs have massive connections to the Internet which means that they can support a very large number of simultaneous users without grinding to a halt. However big is not always best. If there are too many users trying to access the ISP, bottlenecks can occur, resulting in difficulties dialling-in and slower connections during busy periods. Magazines such as *Internet Magazine* publish guides to help you compare the reliability and performance of different ISPs. Back up your research by talking to friends and family already on the Internet – either they will sing the praises of their ISP or recount their frustrations, giving you a fairly good idea how they fare.

What support is available and what are the costs?

Some ISPs only provide support online, while others have 24-hour telephone support, but it is worth researching the charges. Many ISPs, particularly the pay-as-you-go ones, charge a premium call rate for their helpline (sometimes as much as £1 per minute).

'Can you access the ISP using a local telephone number?'

It costs less to connect to the Internet if your ISP can give you a local or low-rate number to call.

'Can you add multiple email accounts? What kind of email addresses are you given?'

Almost all ISPs now allow you to add extra email addresses, for example for other members of a family, without additional charge. Many also offer Web-based email so that you can access your messages from any computer connected to the Internet. Even better are ISPs which allow you something called a *POP3* email address rather than a Web email address. POP3 allows you to use popular email applications to read and write emails without having to be online all the time. This will save you money on your telephone bill.

'Does the ISP provide space for your own Web site? How much space?'

This might be of no importance to you at all, or very important indeed, depending on whether you intend to publish your own Web site and therefore want to take advantage of as much free disk space as possible. Most ISPs provide at least 5Mb free Web space, which will be sufficient, unless you are planning to use lots of audio or video or hundreds of photos.

Chapter **4**

How do I use the World Wide Web?

Getting started

J ust like a library of books and journals, the World Wide Web, or Web for short, enables access to sources of information, called Web sites.

To load and display pages in a Web site you will need a special piece of software called a **Web browser**. If you have a fairly new computer, there is a strong chance that a Web browser will already be installed – Microsoft's

Internet Explorer or Netscape's *Navigator* are the most popular. You will find it on your desktop or by going to the 'Start' menu, selecting 'Programs' and then either 'Internet Explorer' or 'Netscape Communicator' followed by 'Netscape Navigator' (see Fig 4).

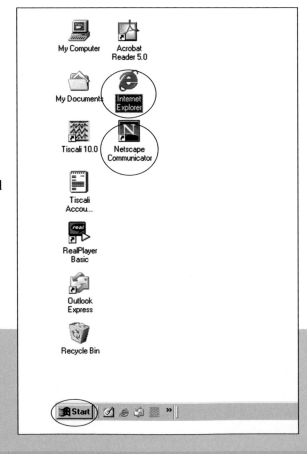

Fig 4 – You can open *Internet Explorer* or *Netscape Navigator* (part of *Netscape Communicator*) from your desktop

If you cannot find a Web browser on your computer, then this free piece of software can be found on the CDs provided by ISPs or often on CDs that come with computer magazines.

New improved versions of these browsers with new features are released from time to time. It is usually best to use the most recent release of a browser, provided that your computer has sufficient memory and speed to support it.

Web browsers differ slightly from each other in the wording and location of menu options and buttons provided (see Figs 5 and 6) but they all perform the same basic functions.

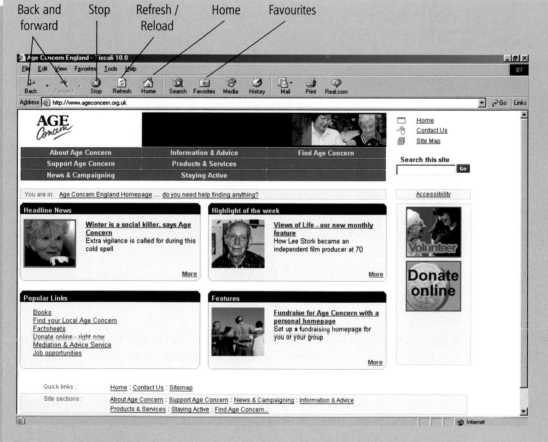

Fig 5 – A typical Web page displayed using *Internet Explorer*

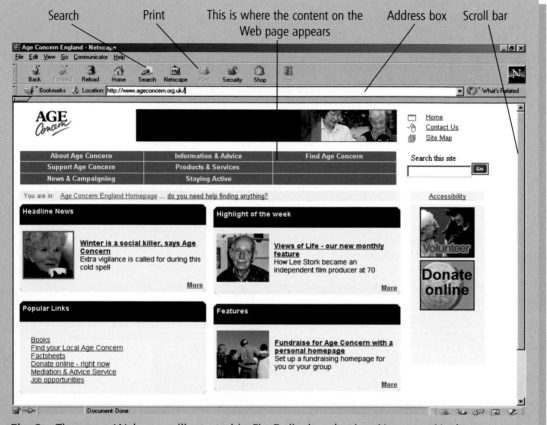

Search   Print   This is where the content on the   Address box   Scroll bar
Web page appears

Fig 6 – The same Web page illustrated in Fig 5 displayed using *Netscape Navigator*.
The menu options are slightly different

These basic functions include the following:

Back/Forward – allow you to retrace your steps and move to pages recently visited.

Stop – allows you to stop loading a page if you clicked on a *hyperlink* by accident or if a page is taking too long to appear.

Refresh/Reload – updates any Web page stored temporarily on the hard disk of your computer with the latest copy of that Web page. This is useful when you return to a page that you've visited recently because your browser will automatically display the page that is stored in the temporary area on your computer's hard disk (the *cache*), rather than the current page on the Web which may have changed in the meantime.

Home – takes you to the page that appears when you first connect to the Internet.

Search – displays a choice of popular *search engines/directories* on the left of your browser screen.

Print – allows you to print the current Web page if your computer is connected to a printer.

The **scroll bar** – click on the scroll bar with your mouse pointer to move up and down a Web page.

Favourites – Web sites that you can save for easy reference later on.

The **address box** – displays the address of the current Web page.

Reading pages on the Web is different from reading pages in a book. Rather than having a single route from one page to the next, you move around a Web site, and between Web sites, by clicking on <u>underlined text</u> and graphics (*hyperlinks*) which link to other pages.

The word 'weather' is a hyperlink

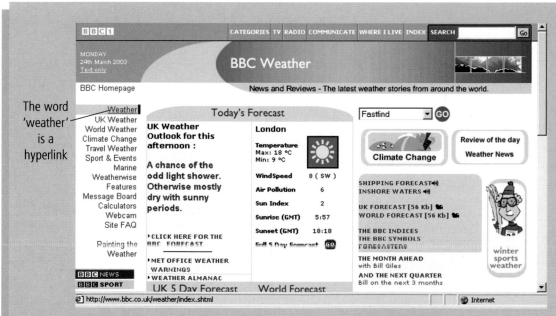

Fig 7 – The BBC Web site (**www.bbc.co.uk**). As the mouse pointer rolls over the word 'weather', the arrow head changes to a hand (not shown) and a message appears in the bottom left-hand corner of the screen indicating the hyperlink's destination page

You can always spot where the hyperlinks are on a Web page because if they are text, the text is usually underlined or displayed in a different colour to the rest of the text. Also, as you move your mouse pointer over a hyperlink, the pointer changes shape to look more like a pointing hand 🖑 and the title of the destination page is often displayed in the bottom left of your browser (see Fig 7).

Common questions

'What happens if I turn off my computer while I am still connected to the Internet?'

There is no need to worry, you won't be running up a huge telephone bill just because you forgot to click on 'disconnect' before switching off your computer. Closing down your computer automatically disconnects you from the Internet.

'The text is too small for me to read properly. Can I make it bigger?'

You only need to make a couple of simple changes in your browser settings to increase or decrease the size of text to make it easier to read.

If you are using *Internet Explorer*, click on 'View' at the very top of your browser window and select 'Text Size'. A drop-down menu will appear. From this select 'largest' through to 'smallest' to increase/decrease the size of the text.

If you are using *Navigator*, click on 'View' at the very top of your browser window. Select 'Increase font size' or 'Decrease font size'.

You may find that changing the font size distorts graphic and text alignments in some pages, in which case you can always change the font size again until you are satisfied with the balance between readability and page layout.

'I have trouble with some colours – can I control the colour settings of Web pages myself?'

You can make a simple change to your Web browser to change the colour settings to make Web pages easier to read.

To change colour settings using *Internet Explorer*, select the 'Tools' menu, then 'Internet Options', then 'General' and finally select 'Colour'.

To change colour settings using *Navigator,* select the 'Edit' menu, then 'Preferences', then 'Appearance' and finally select 'Colour'.

Some Web sites, however, are designed in such a way that your Web browser will not be able to override its colour settings.

'Why do I sometimes have to wait a long time for pictures on Web pages to appear?'

Web pages can consist of many individual elements – menu bars, logos, advertisements, photographs, etc – which load one at a time and build up a Web page like a jigsaw. If your connection to the Internet slows down, which often happens at peak times when many other people are attempting to connect to the Internet through the same ISP or connect to the same page as you, then these Web page elements will take much longer to load and display on your computer.

'Can I change the page that appears first when I connect to the Internet?'

Yes – go to the page that you want to appear when you first connect to the Internet to check the Web address. If you are using *Internet Explorer*, select 'Internet Options' from the 'Tools' menu. If you are using *Netscape Navigator*, select 'Preferences' from the 'Edit' menu. Type in the Web address of the page, then click on the button labelled 'Use Current' or 'Use Current Page' (see Fig 8). Now when you click on the 'Home' button on your browser, this page will automatically load.

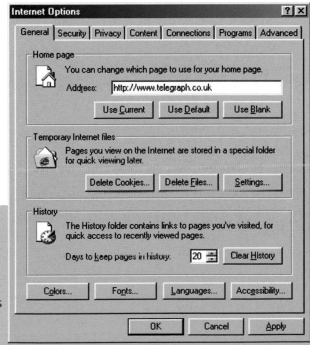

Fig 8 – Select a Web address to be the new home page; for example *The Telegraph*

Searching the Web

Many people find that it is fun to explore the Web by surfing from site to site, going wherever the hyperlinks take them. But when you are trying to find something specific, and find it as soon as possible, you will need to go through a process of searching for the information you are after, and on the Web you have two approach paths. You can either search directly by address or by using the equivalent of a telephone directory.

Web addresses

If you look carefully at the posters on a bus, or the adverts in a newspaper, or the next letter from your bank, the chances are that you will find reference somewhere to a ***Web address*** as a way of finding out more information. For many businesses a Web address is as important as a telephone or fax number.

These Web addresses (or ***Universal Resource Locators – URLs –*** which is their more technical but far less descriptive name) look complex and must be typed in with care so as not to make any typing errors or leave any characters out.

To visit a Web site via its Web address, you simply type in the address into the address box and press the 'Return' key on your keyboard.

If you understand the components of a Web address it can help you understand more about the site you visit. Web addresses typically look something like this:

http://www.bbc.co.uk

http://www – This part tells your Web browser that it is looking for a Web site. The 'www' literally stands for 'World Wide Web'. Most Web browsers allow you to 'drop' the 'http://' so that you only need to type www.bbc.co.uk

bbc – This is the name of the Web site itself.

.co – This part describes the kind of Web site it is. .co indicates a company. Other common ones you may encounter are .org to indicate a not-for-profit organisation and .gov to indicate government. The 'dot' itself is very important and is typed in using the full-stop character on your keyboard.

.uk – This part describes the country of origin. Again, the 'dot' is important and must not be missed out.

Search engines and directories

If you do not have the right Web address to hand, or you just want to conduct a more general search, then you can type in a word or phrase to describe the topic you are interested in into a search engine or directory, just as you might use a telephone directory to track down a club or business.

No search tool could keep track of all the content on the Internet. They all put together their lists of sites in different ways. Search directories rely on the 'human touch' (ie people who look at individual Web pages manually and categorise them). Search engines use intelligent software to index Web pages using keywords taken from the pages.

There are hundreds of search engines and directories on offer. Your ISP will either provide a list or suggest one that you can access from the 'Search' button on your Web browser. Alternatively, if you know the Web address of one you like using, type it into the Address box and press the 'Enter' key or 'Return' key on your keyboard in the usual way.

Finding a needle in a haystack: tips for better searching

The volume of information available on the Web can work against you if you are trying to find something specific and have to wade through pages and pages before you get to one that looks vaguely useful or interesting, so follow these guidelines which may help to reduce the number of false leads:

1 Pick a search engine or directory to suit

If you are looking for a broad, general topic, such as where to find cheap holidays, use a search directory compiled by humans such as Yahoo! because it tends to list fewer results of higher quality. If you're looking for a slightly rarer topic, such as 19th-century quilting, use a search engine that may be less precise but lists more, such as AltaVista.

How to choose a search engine

Google – www.google.co.uk

Currently the most popular search engine. It combs the Internet on a regular basis to bring you new Web sites and updates to Web sites. It offers clean, uncluttered Web pages and is very fast. Google also features a button called 'I'm Feeling Lucky' which takes you directly to the Web page which most closely fits your search request.

Ask Jeeves – www.ask.co.uk

Allows you to ask your question in plain English – for example 'What is the exchange rate for the Spanish peseta?'. You then get a list of related questions and by clicking on the one you want you will be taken to a Web page that may provide you with the right answer.

AltaVista UK – www.altavista.co.uk

Maintains a massive index, which means that it is useful for broad searching and for offbeat subjects.

Lycos – www.lycos.co.uk

Lycos has been around since the early days of the Internet and is still one of the most popular search engines. Like AltaVista, it is good for finding more specific information in pages of a Web site.

Excite – www.excite.co.uk

Like AltaVista, it is good for finding more specific information in pages of a Web site.

Meta Crawler – www.metacrawler.com

Rather than keeping its own catalogue of Web sites, MetaCrawler conducts your search simultaneously on several search engines at once. This means it can be a little slower, but it is likely to retrieve more accurate results.

Yahoo! UK – www.yahoo.co.uk

The largest human-compiled guide to the Web, which means it is good for identifying general information on a broad topic as it organises the Web into subjects and categories such as Arts, Education, Entertainment, Government, Health, News and Recreation. Yahoo! works well if you are looking for information that fits neatly into an obvious subject or category. It also provides the choice whether to search the whole of the Web or only UK sites.

BBC – www.bbc.co.uk

The BBC's search engine is based on Google search technology. Search results are clear, uncluttered, relevant, and free of advertisements.

MSN – www.msn.co.uk

Microsoft's MSN service features both directory listings and one of the most powerful search engines.

2 Narrow down your search by geography

Many search tools offer the facility to search the entire Web or to limit the search to information with a UK bias; for example Google – **www.google.co.uk**. It may be useful to expand your search for general research purposes, but limit your site when you are looking for local information.

3 Watch your spelling

Sometimes your search will be fruitless because it has been spelt incorrectly. Luckily Google has a spellchecker, so if you type in '**cathederal**' for example it will ask you '**Did you mean cathedral?**'.

4 Be persistent and creative

Often on the Internet it does not matter whether you use capital or lower-case letters. When you are searching, however, it's best to use capital letters for names of people, places and titles.

If you enter just one keyword into your search you'll end up with far too many results. You can make searches more specific by typing two or more words and surrounding them with speech marks (" ") or by joining them with **AND**, **+**, **a comma**, or **&**. This can be useful when searching for a phrase, or person or film title. For example, just entering the word '**bridge**' delivers thousands of results, whereas a search on '**bridge+card+game**' lists a far more specific set of results (see Figs 9–10).

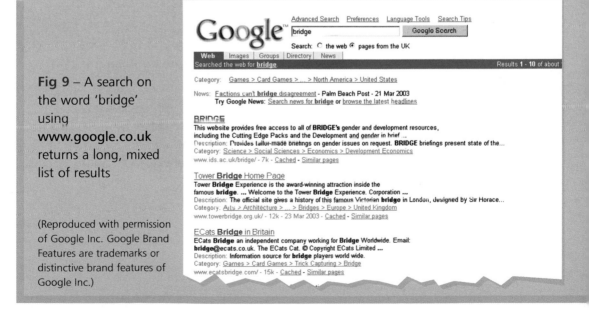

Fig 9 – A search on the word 'bridge' using **www.google.co.uk** returns a long, mixed list of results

(Reproduced with permission of Google Inc. Google Brand Features are trademarks or distinctive brand features of Google Inc.)

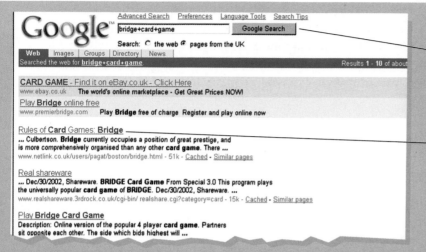

Re-enter your search word or phrase then click the button 'Search' (sometimes labelled 'Go' or 'Go Get It')

The title also acts as a hyperlink, so to look at a page, click on the title with your mouse pointer. The description enables you to assess whether the page is worthy of a closer look

Fig 10 – A more descriptive search phrase such as 'bridge+card+game' returns more useful results

(Reproduced with permission of Google Inc. Google Brand Features are trademarks or distinctive brand features of Google Inc.)

5 Read the help

The techniques mentioned above vary between search tools. Get to know the one you like best by reading the 'advanced' sections.

Understanding search results

To view any of the Web pages returned from your search, click on the page title which usually appears in **blue underlined text**. The paragraph of text beneath the page title usually gives you a little more information about the contents.

It can help to keep the search results page open, while opening Web pages you choose from this page (known as opening a separate window). Click on the page title with the **right** mouse button and a pop-up menu will appear. Revert back to your **left** mouse button and click 'Open link in new window'.

To move between windows click on the one you want from the 'Taskbar' at the bottom of your screen, or hold down the 'Alt' key and tap the 'Tab' key on your keyboard until you reach the window you want, then release.

Opening multiple windows will slow down your computer, so it is good practice to close the additional windows after you have finished with them.

Bookmarking favourite Web sites

Once you have found a page that you like you can tag it for future reference. This means that you never need to remember the route you took to find the page again, or the Web address of the page itself.

Web browsers vary slightly in the way they allow you to tag a Web page, and they use different names for this feature. In *Internet Explorer* select 'Favourites' from the menu. In *Netscape Navigator* select 'Bookmarks' from the menu.

Tips

1 Edit the text that is used to describe your Favourite. Text contained in the Web page will automatically be suggested, but change it if you think it is not very helpful.

2 If you create a lot of Favourites, it can also be useful to organise them into logical categories (called 'folders'). You can decide what these categories should be called – for example you might have a set of Favourites organised within a 'travel' category.

3 Tidy up your Favourites once in a while by deleting them, especially if a Web page you previously tagged no longer exists or is no longer relevant.

4 If you save a Web page as a Favourite with the 'Make available offline' box ticked (✓), you will not have to be online to view the page in future. Remember, however, that the links you follow from that page will not be available without going online.

Common questions

'What is meant by a 'dot com?' I hear the term a lot in relation to the Internet.'

The term literally means '.com'. A large proportion of Web addresses end with .com (short for 'company') – for example www.lastminute.com

'Is there a simple way to revisit a Web page?'

Surfing the Web is like a journey and your Web browser will remember your route. At any stage in your journey you can retrace your steps. To move sequentially back through the pages you have visited recently, use the 'Back' and 'Forward' buttons in your browser menu. To jump straight to a particular page, click the down-pointing arrow at the end of the address box to select from the list of pages, or use the 'History' tool. In *Internet Explorer*, select the 'Tools' menu followed by 'History' – the pages will be listed in the left-hand pane of your browser screen (see Fig 11). In *Netscape Navigator*, select the 'Communicator' menu, followed by 'Tools', followed by 'History'.

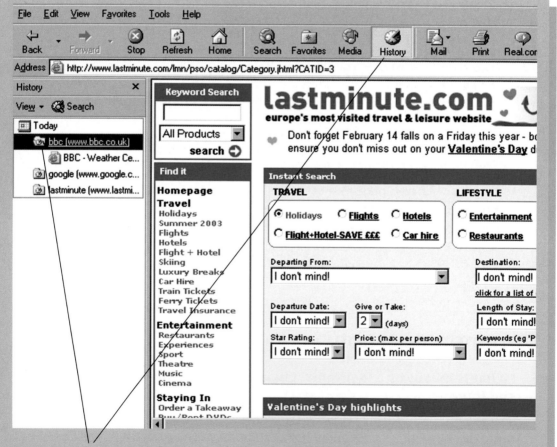

Fig 11 – Retrace your steps by selecting 'History' and then pick a page from the list in the left-hand pane of Web pages that you have visited recently

Chapter **5**

How can I send and receive emails?

Email is a cheap way of sending a message to someone – even if you are sending it to Australia, you only pay the cost of a local telephone call and the cost doesn't increase with size (a weighty 100-page document will cost the same as a single line of text).

The information about who an email message is for and how they can be located is all wrapped up within the ***email address***.

When you sign up with an Internet Service Provider (ISP) you will be given an email account and will have the opportunity to choose or change your email address. You may have heard an email address given out on a radio or television programme and puzzled over the meaning of the strange-sounding expressions. A typical email address looks something like this:
heatherbloggs@hotmail.com

heatherbloggs is the unique name that you choose for your email address. Sometimes names are separated by a full-stop; for example
heather.bloggs

@ is pronounced 'at'.

hotmail.com is the name of your ISP or whoever is providing your email address (in this example hotmail), and is pronounced 'hotmail **dot** com'.

Sending an email

1 Start up your email program

The most popular email program is *Outlook Express* which is part of *Internet Explorer*. You will find your email program on your desktop. Alternatively, you can go to the 'Start' menu, select 'Programs' then 'Outlook Express'.

Email programs, like Web browsers, differ slightly from each other but they all perform the same basic functions shown in Fig 12.

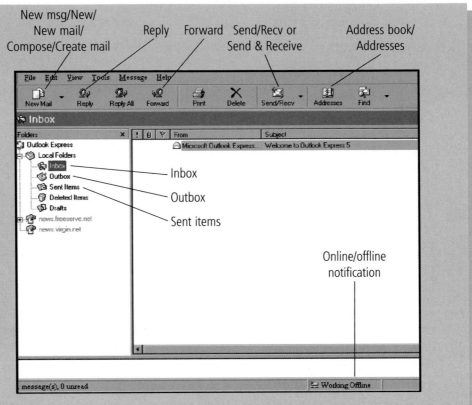

Fig 12 – The main functions and features of an email program
(*Outlook Express*)

Inbox – Lists all the emails you have received.

Outbox – Emails waiting to be sent will be stored here temporarily.

Sent Items – Emails which have been sent are listed here.

New msg/New/New mail/Compose/Create mail – Start a new message.

Reply – Reply to a message that you have received.

Forward – Send the message on to another person.

Address book/Addresses – Add/remove/amend email addresses in your address book.

Send/Recv or **Send & Receive** – Make a connection to the Internet to send any email messages in your Outbox and receive any new messages that have been sent to you.

Your email program may immediately try to connect you to the Internet, but the only time that you actually need to make a connection is when you finally come to send your completed email, so for the time being stop the connection being made (for example click 'cancel' or 'work offline').

2 | Create a new message

To compose a new message, click on the button labelled either 'New mail', 'New msg', 'New' or 'Compose'.

3 | Enter the email address

In the box labelled 'To', type in the email address of the person you are sending the email to. If this is someone that you regularly email, you will find the 'address book' facility useful because it allows you to keep a record of the email addresses you use frequently and then pick out these email addresses when you are creating a new message (see Fig 13).

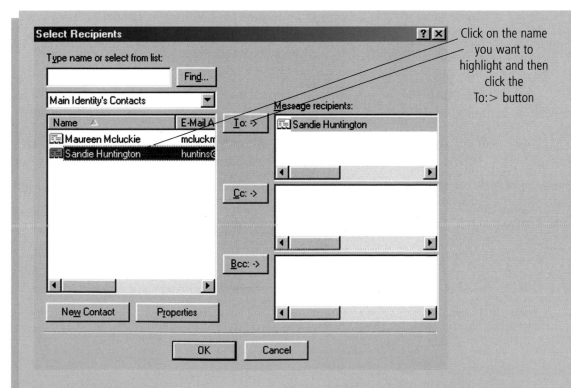

Fig 13 – Use the address book to pick out email addresses which you use frequently

You can also send a copy of the message to another person at the same time, by typing in their email address, or adding it from your address book, in the box labelled 'Cc' (Cc stands for 'Carbon copy').

If you want to send a copy of your email to someone else in secret, then type in their email address, or add it from your address book, in the box labelled 'Bcc' (short for 'Blind carbon copy'). That person will receive the message, but their email address will not appear in the list of recipients, so the other person or people it has been sent to will be unaware of this additional recipient.

4 Type in the subject of your email

In the box labelled 'Subject', type in a short phrase or a single word to describe your message. This subject will appear in the recipient's email Inbox.

5 Write your message

Your message can be as long or as short as you like, as formal or informal as you want to be. One good idea is to check over your spelling before you send your message by selecting the spellchecking option from the 'Tools' menu (or directly from the toolbar if available).

Fig 14 – Writing an email using *Outlook Express*

You can also send ('attach') files from your computer together with your text message. This is ideal for sending something like a scanned photograph or a more detailed letter or report electronically.

Simply click on the button labelled 'Attach' (sometimes pictured as a paperclip ✐) and then browse through the files and folders on your computer until you find the document you want to attach.

6 | Send your message

You can send your message as soon as you finish writing it by clicking on the button labelled 'Send' to make a connection with your ISP.

Alternatively, you can save your message by selecting 'File' followed by 'Send Later' – they will be kept in your Outbox until you are ready to go online and then all will be sent at once. Sending 20 messages like this will cost about the same as sending one!

To ensure that when you start to use *Outlook Express* you work offline (and therefore choose for yourself when you wish to make a connection to your ISP to go online), go to the *Outlook Express* 'Tools' menu, select 'Options' and go to the 'General' tab. Ensure that the 'Send and receive messages at startup' box does *not* have a tick (✓) in it.

How does it work?

When you make a connection to your ISP and send an email, your message is sent down the telephone line to a huge computer managed by your ISP called a **mail server**. At this point you can disconnect from your ISP. The ISP's mail server then sends the message to its final destination which is coded within the email address.

Receiving an email

Receiving and responding to an email is much simpler. First you must connect to your ISP, start up your email program and click on the button labelled 'Send/Recv' or 'Send & Receive'. Any new email messages that have been sent to you will appear in your Inbox. You can then disconnect from your ISP at this point.

To read a message, open up your Inbox and double-click on the message you want to open.

If you want to reply, click on the button labelled 'Reply'. A new message box will be opened which automatically contains the email address of the person who has sent you the message and contains the same subject name preceded with the letters 'Re' to indicate that it is a reply. Enter your message, and then send your reply.

Be aware, however, that sending a reply will mean that your response, together with the additional message, will be sent back to the other person. If it was a large file it could result in an unnecessarily long internet connection, so remember to delete any unnecessary text/attachments in your email message that you do not want to send with your reply.

When you open your Inbox you will be able to spot at a glance any emails that have been sent with an attached file. The Attachments symbol (📎) will appear next to the message. With the message open you can double-click on the attachment to open it. You can also save the attachment to a folder on your own computer by clicking on the attachment with the **right** mouse button or selecting 'Save All Attachments' (which is sometimes hidden away in the 'File' menu).

Emails will be stored in your Inbox until you choose to move or delete them.

As you build up an assorted collection of email messages, you may find it helpful to organise your messages into folders. To create a new folder select 'New' from the 'File' menu and 'Folder' and type in a name for the new folder. You can then highlight any of the messages currently in your Inbox and drag them into this new folder.

*H*ow does it work?

When someone sends an email message to you, it is stored on your ISP's mail server until you request it. When you make a connection to your ISP, the message is sent down your telephone line to your computer via your modem (this is known as '*downloading*') and is stored in your email Inbox.

*C*ommon questions

'How can I minimise the amount of time I spend online when using email?'

You do not need to be online to read or write an email – only when you want to send or receive a message. So when you receive an email, disconnect from your ISP and read your message at leisure. You can even set *Outlook Express* to disconnect from your ISP immediately after it has completed the Send and Receive, so you don't have to remember to do it yourself. From the 'Tools' menu, select 'Options' and click on the 'Connection' tab. Ensure that the 'Hang-up after sending and receiving' box has a tick (✓) against it.

'Will I still be able to receive emails even if I switch off my computer?'

Yes. An email isn't actually transmitted directly to your computer: instead it is held by your ISP in space that they 'reserve' on their mail server for your email messages – it's just like having your own pigeon-hole. It is only when you connect to your ISP and click on the 'Send/Recv' button that any emails in your 'pigeon-hole' are downloaded to your Inbox.

'Can I send and receive emails on any computer?'

Yes, but you will need to set up a Web email account such as a 'hotmail' account (so-called because your email address will take the form yourname@hotmail.com). To set up a 'hotmail' account go to the Web site **www.hotmail.co.uk** Once you have set up a Web email account you can go to any computer connected to the Internet (imagine for example going on holiday and keeping in touch with family and friends by email), visit the same Web site, enter your username and password and send and receive emails using that account. These email accounts are free but the disadvantage is that all the while you are writing your message or reading your emails you are online, time is ticking and the telephone bill is mounting.

'My friend has sent me an email with an attachment but when I open up the attached document it is completely unreadable. Why is this?'

Don't worry – you are not doing anything wrong. This happens when someone sends you a document which has been created using software that you are not running on your own computer, or a different *version* of the software to the one you are using on your own computer. As a result your computer cannot interpret the document and either cannot open the document at all or, in trying to interpret it, scrambles the contents. The best thing to do is to contact your friend, resolve whether they are trying to send you a document that you simply will not be able to open because you do not have the right piece of software, or whether you do have the software but will need the file to be saved as a different version and then be sent again.

'How do I know that my email has been sent successfully?'

To check that a message has left your computer, open up your 'Sent' folder. The message should appear in the list (at the top of the list if it is sorted by date).

If your email was not correctly addressed – for example you misspelled the person's name or typed a comma by mistake into the email address – then you will be sent a failure message to inform you that the email was not delivered. If the mistake is obvious, correct it and send the email again. If you are writing an email and are unsure whether you have a correct email address, you could end your message by asking the person to reply back to you to acknowledge that they have received it. Allow them a little bit of time to reply, and if they don't, then try again or find another way to contact them.

Chapter 6

How can I go shopping on the Internet?

Shopping on the Internet, sometimes referred to as *e-commerce*, can be a blissful experience – sitting down with a cup of coffee or tea to hand, you are a long way from the jostling crowds, the long queues, busy car parks and pickpockets. Come rain or shine, night or day, this virtual marketplace is open for business.

You might be feeling a little nervous about shopping on the Internet, and this is very natural since you cannot see or feel the goods that you are buying or meet the shopkeepers face to face. But by being aware of possible hazards and areas where you need to tread carefully, shopping on the Internet should be no more risky than buying by mail order or over the telephone.

Choosing where to shop

The Internet gives you a shopping window onto a world of goods and services which aren't always readily available on the high street. But it's more important than ever to know who you are dealing with, because on the Internet it is a lot easier for unscrupulous companies to conceal their identities.

Find your feet by exploring some of the Web sites of well-known retailers first. Make intelligent guesses at their Web addresses or type in the names of the companies into a search engine.

Retailers

The Web addresses of well-known retailers tend to be based on their company names. Some examples include:

www.argos.co.uk	www.marksandspencer.com
www.bandq.co.uk	www.sainsburys.co.uk
www.boots.co.uk	www.tesco.com
www.debenhams.com	www.whsmith.co.uk
www.iceland.co.uk	www.lloydspharmacy.com

Internet shopping checklist

1 Make sure you know who the company or person is behind the Web site, and if in doubt look up their telephone number and address and call them in person to double-check their details (be wary of any site which does not give you full contact details).

2 Check where the company is based. If it is outside the UK, you may want to avoid buying very expensive items from them, unless you know them well, to limit the risk of things going wrong or possible additional expenses, such as the cost of returning goods.

3 A Web site that is up to date and professionally designed tends to fill you with more confidence about the retailer than a site which looks as if it has been put together in a teenager's bedroom. But fight the temptation to judge a retailer by its appearance alone; an enticing Web site is no guarantee that the company will deliver on its promises.

4 If you haven't heard of a company, see if any family or friends know of it. Also look out for the TrustUK logo (see Fig 15) which means that the company is a member of a trade association or subscribes to a strict code of practice.

5 Any Web retailer should enable you to send your credit card details via secure pages which encrypt the details as they are transmitted. Only buy from Web retailers offering this facility.

Fig 15 – Look out for the TrustUK logo on retailer Web sites

Coming up with the goods

Sites usually have comprehensive information about products, including pictures, prices and descriptions. Some actually give you more detail than shops do, for example by including reviews, and suggestions for other related items.

You will have to go through some kind of selection process to find the things that you want to buy, down to details such as size and colour, depending on the type of product. Many sites provide a search facility which allows you to enter the product, brand name or service you are looking for. But if you are in the mood for browsing, then most sites will also provide you with a series of menus to help you get to what you want.

Simple sites will expect you to make a note of product names and prices as you go along so that you can fill in an order form. More sophisticated sites will give you a 'virtual shopping basket' into which you place all the items that you have selected to buy and then invite you to the 'checkout', where the contents of your 'basket' are turned into an order (see Fig 16).

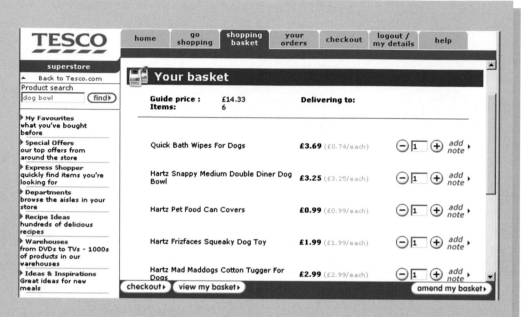

Fig 16 – To select items from the Tesco online superstore (**www.tesco.com**), add them to your shopping basket, and at any time check your basket to list everything you have picked

Reading the small print

As with all purchases, read the small print to make sure that there are no nasty surprises waiting for you. Look carefully at the price of what you are buying (especially if you have to convert from a price quoted in a different currency) and watch for additional, sometimes hidden, charges such as VAT, high delivery rates (particularly from overseas), packaging, taxes or duties and any extra charges for using a particular payment method.

Before you finally complete the order, read the Terms and Conditions on the retailer's Web site. Check the refund and return policies, what protections are offered in case things go wrong, how long delivery will take and, if the facility is offered on the site, the current stock level.

You should also read the retailer's privacy policy statement so that you are aware of what personal information they intend to collect and what they are going to do with it. There should always be the opportunity to opt out of any scheme which would pass on your personal information to other companies.

Making the payment

How often do you hand your credit card to a waiter in a restaurant or give out your account number over the telephone? These transactions probably pose a greater security risk than giving out your credit card details online.

When you have checked your order and are ready to make the payment, check that the page you are on is secure. Often a message will flash up on your screen to announce that you are entering a secure page; most importantly you should look out for a closed padlock symbol in the status bar at the bottom of your browser screen which shows that your details are protected when being sent (see Fig 17).

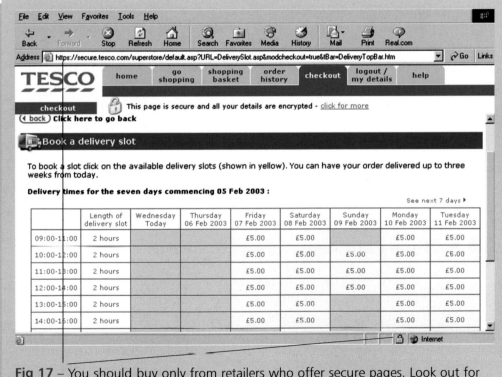

Fig 17 – You should buy only from retailers who offer secure pages. Look out for the padlock symbol and a Web address beginning 'https://...'

As a last precaution, when you have finally placed your order, save copies of the information relating to the transaction, including a copy of the completed order form, order number, and copies of any email correspondence that you have with the retailer. If you have a printer you can print this information out (select 'print' from your browser), or save a copy of this Web page to your computer by selecting the 'File' menu followed by 'Save As'.

Any good retailer will email you to acknowledge and summarise your order, giving you a unique reference number to use in any further correspondence.

An example – www.amazon.co.uk

1 Find the right Web site

More people buy books on the Internet than any other item, and there are many Web sites selling books, enabling you to shop around for the cheapest prices. A very successful online retailer, which sells books among other things, is a company called *Amazon*.

Amazon first started in America with www.amazon.com It then expanded to Europe and established a UK site – www.amazon.co.uk This led to many confused UK shoppers buying from the American site by mistake, adding to the cost of their orders due to additional expenses such as overseas postage.

Therefore, if you are browsing for something to buy on a site which is not specifically aimed at the UK market then look out for a signpost to a UK-only site, or enquire if there is one.

2 Find the right item

You will need to go through a process of searching the site to find the item(s) that you want. In this case, *Amazon* provides a useful search box which allows you to specify the name of a book, author or a keyword to trace the book that you want (see Fig 18).

3 Inspect the item

Once you have found an item, find out more about it by reading a description of it, or zoom in to inspect a more descriptive photograph of it (see Fig 19). At this stage you should also look into the full price of the item, details of the retailer's refund and return policies and, where possible, product reviews and an idea of current stock levels or how long it will take to deliver the item to your door.

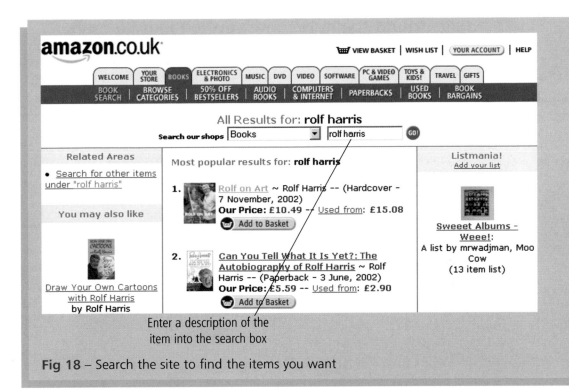

Enter a description of the
item into the search box

Fig 18 – Search the site to find the items you want

Look at the
description, the
price, the
availability,
reviews etc, to
help you decide
whether to buy
or not

If you're
satisfied, add it
to your shopping
basket

Fig 19 – Find out all the details you can about the items you want

4 | You've found the item, now you're ready to buy

The Web site should give you the opportunity to inspect the items in your shopping basket at any time, update any of them or take any out that you have since changed your mind about. When you are satisfied that you have everything you want, you then proceed to the checkout (see Fig 20).

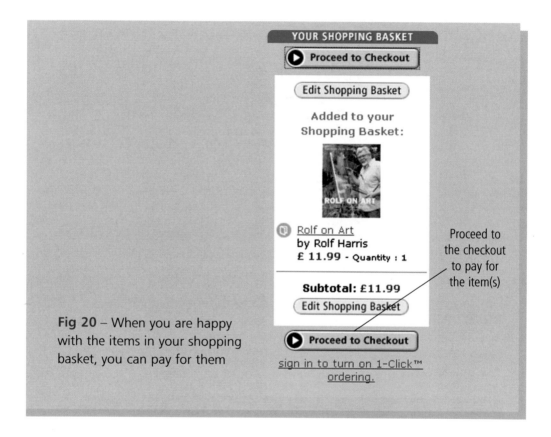

YOUR SHOPPING BASKET

▶ Proceed to Checkout

(Edit Shopping Basket)

Added to your
Shopping Basket:

ROLF ON ART

🔊 Rolf on Art
by Rolf Harris
£ 11.99 - Quantity : 1

Subtotal: £11.99

(Edit Shopping Basket)

▶ Proceed to Checkout

sign in to turn on 1-Click™
ordering.

Proceed to
the checkout
to pay for
the item(s)

Fig 20 – When you are happy with the items in your shopping basket, you can pay for them

5 | Time to pay

When you are ready to pay, you will be asked to select a payment method and provide your credit card number, expiry date and, for some cards, the issue number and start date. Remember to look out for signs that the current Web page is secure. **You should not give out your credit card details unless the page is secure** (as shown in Fig 21).

You will also need to give your name, email address, postal address and delivery address, and may be invited to register, so that if you visit the site again you will not have to retype all your details.

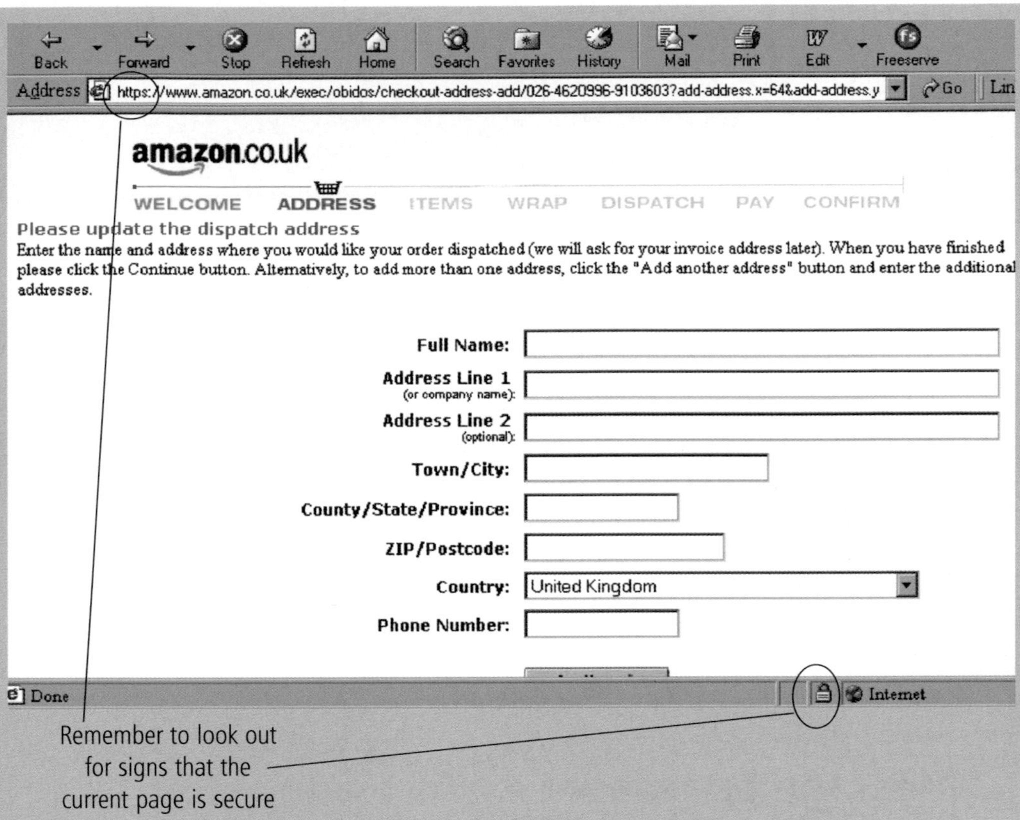

Remember to look out
for signs that the
current page is secure

Fig 21 – Check that the page is secure before paying

6 Confirmation of order

At the end of the process you will be asked to confirm the details you have given, and then the sale is complete. Any good retailer will also confirm your order by email with a reference number, so that you can track its progress.

Chapter 7

How can I chat to people on the Internet?

A problem shared is a problem halved, particularly if you can find half a dozen other people to share it with. So whether you simply want to track down someone who can help you answer a question that has been plaguing you for days, or you are embarking on a new venture and could do with some handy hints from people who have relevant experience, or you have a passion for a new hobby that you are eager to share, the Internet provides access to worldwide communities of people who share your interests, have been through similar experiences, or have interesting tales to tell.

Message boards

One of the easiest ways to share your views on a subject is using a message board. Message boards (also called 'bulletin boards') are typically pages in Web sites which invite you to post up a message that other people can see and reply to. They are a useful way of sharing advice and tips with wide groups of people.

The BBC Web site includes message boards for some of its popular television programmes such as *Gardeners' World* (**www.bbc.co.uk/gardening** – see Fig 22) in which you might see messages from people sharing tips on tackling garden pests, for example.

Fig 22 – The BBC's gardening message board (www.bbc.co.uk/gardening) is popular and easy to use

Mailing lists

You sign up to join a mailing list simply by supplying an email address and a password. The idea is that anyone on the list can send a message which is then sent out to everyone else on the list by email. Messages are normally also published to a message board on a Web page which captures all the messages that have been sent to the mailing list on the subject. In turn anyone on the list can comment on the message, replying by email or by visiting the Web page.

Sometimes it is also possible to opt to receive updates as a 'digest', which saves you being overwhelmed with a daily flood of emails; you simply receive a periodic summary of the messages. You may also find it helpful to create a new folder into which you can save any of these messages that you wish to keep for future reference.

If you go away on holiday, it might be a good idea to temporarily unsubscribe, just as you would temporarily stop your newspaper delivery, because a mailing list which is particularly popular will generate many hundreds of messages a day which could overload your mailbox.

Web sites such as http://groups.yahoo.co.uk (see Fig 23) provide mailing lists that you can join. If you don't find any that suit, they also provide a simple way to set up your own.

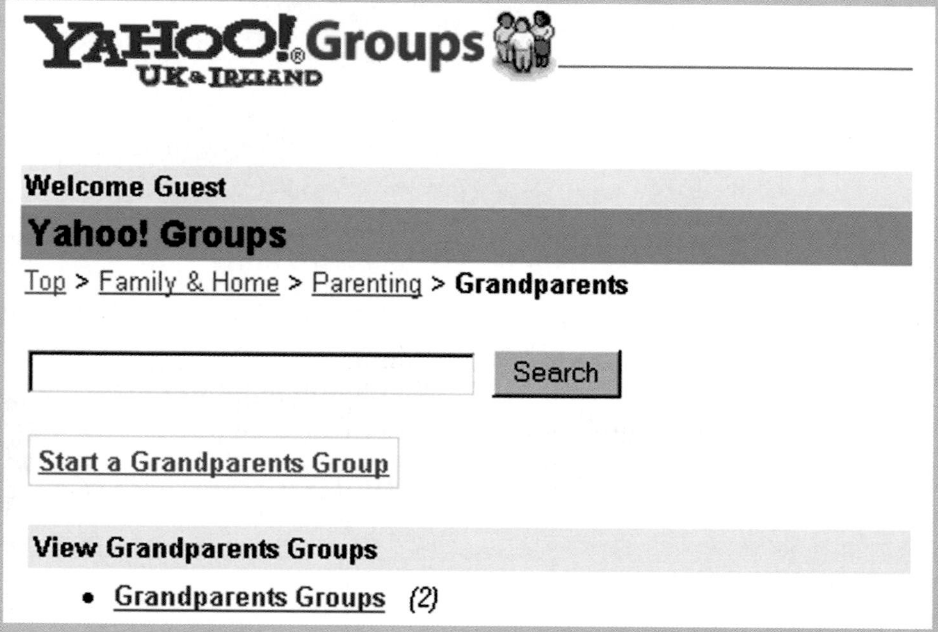

Fig 23 – An example of a grandparenting mailing list Web site – http://groups.yahoo.co.uk

Newsgroups

Newsgroups are collections of public messages on large computers called *news servers*. You can find newsgroups on practically any subject; they are organised into subject hierarchies, with the first few letters of the newsgroup name indicating the subject category. Each subject has many levels of sub-topics. Subject categories include: news, rec (recreation), soc (society), sci (science), comp (computers), but there are many more.

You can access a newsgroup using Web browsers like *Internet Explorer* and *Netscape Navigator* or using email programs like *Outlook Express* and *Netscape Messenger*. Webs sites like Google Groups (http://groups.google.co.uk) allow you to look at newsgroups without any special software – you can just use your Web browser (see Fig 24).

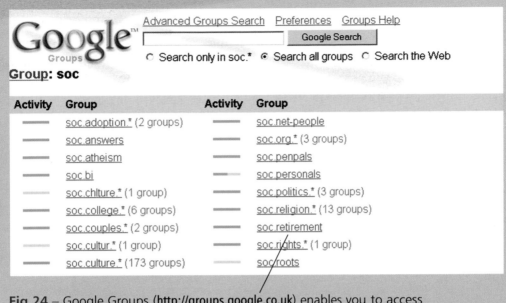

Fig 24 – Google Groups (http://groups.google.co.uk) enables you to access newsgroups on a chosen subject, such as retirement

(Reproduced with permission of Google Inc.Google Brand Features are trademarks or distinctive brand features of Google Inc.)

To read or participate in a newsgroup you have to give a membership name, password and email address. The messages are presented in a list, known as a 'thread', which shows the original message, the responses to the message, and the responses to the responses, so you can follow an entire conversation or just the sections you are interested in.

Some newsgroups are moderated by a person who decides which messages to allow or to remove, but most newsgroups are unmoderated, so people are free to add just about anything they like.

As with other spaces where people spend time, there are rules of polite behaviour when using newsgroups which you are expected to observe. Before you participate in a newsgroup you should spend a little time learning the purpose and the 'rules' of the newsgroup before posting any messages of your own. They can be quite intimidating to the first time user.

Chat sites

Unlike mailing lists and newsgroups, chat sites offer a way to hold conversations in 'real time', in a similar way to having a telephone conversation with a number of people at the same time, except that you type instead of talk.

You need to register to become a member of a chat site and to think of a nickname, which will be the name by which people will know you and address you inside the chat site. Some chat sites invite you to provide a little bit of information about yourself. This is useful if you are keen to meet people with a similar interest, or you want to promote a society or club that you belong to. However, remember that things may not always be as they seem – it is very easy to pretend to be someone else on the Internet, so be cautious about giving out too much personal information.

The number of chat sites is growing all the time so it shouldn't be too difficult to find one that you feel comfortable with and that covers topics that interest you.

Try typing in a set of search words (such as 'family + history + chat') into a search engine to find a chat site which covers a topic that you are interested in, or try a chat site like Yahoo! Chat (http://uk.chat.yahoo.com) which offers hundreds of chat rooms.

Age Concern offers a very popular chat site called the Baby Boomer Bistro (www.bbb.org.uk – see Fig 25), for lively chat and themed discussions on subjects such as genealogy, music, recipes and gardening.

Fig 25 – Age Concern offers a very popular chat site called the Baby Boomer Bistro (www.bbb.org.uk). Go through a simple registration process and then you're ready to chat

Chapter 8

How can the Internet help me research my family history?

Researching family history is one of the most popular internet hobbies. Thousands and thousands more people every year are finding that the Internet can help them in their quest to discover more about their roots.

Making a start

The first step in researching your family history is to gather as many old photographs, documents, names, places and dates from family friends and relatives as you can. The next steps, however, are often less clear, especially when so many Web sites are on offer, dedicated to providing help and advice on tracing your roots.

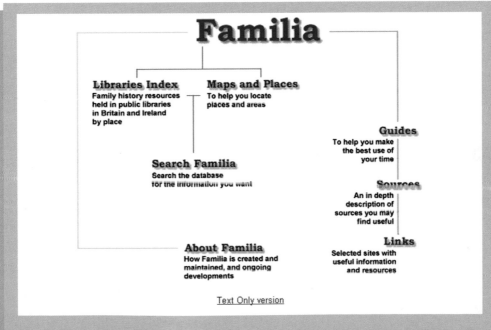

Fig 26 – The Familia Web site (www.familia.org.uk) tells you what family history research resources are available in the public libraries of the UK and Ireland

Public libraries and record offices will be useful if you are researching a particular area of the country. A Web site called 'Familia' at www.familia.org.uk (see Fig 26) can save you some leg-work by listing the type of family history research resources available in the public libraries of the UK and Ireland.

A Web site called 'FreeBMD' (which stands for Free Births, Marriages and Deaths) at http://freebmd.rootsweb.com/ provides internet access to millions of UK birth, marriage and death records covering the period 1837–1902.

If you are after a hard copy of a birth, marriage or death certificate, the Web site of the General Register Office for England and Wales at www.statistics.gov.uk/registration can also save you some time by allowing you to download an application form to obtain copies of certificates by post. The Register Offices for Scotland and Northern Ireland also have equivalent Web sites.

Parish registers are useful for tracing baptisms, marriages and burials, especially those that date before the introduction of civil registration. The Web site of the Society of Genealogists at www.sog.org.uk lists the copies of parish registers held in the Society's library.

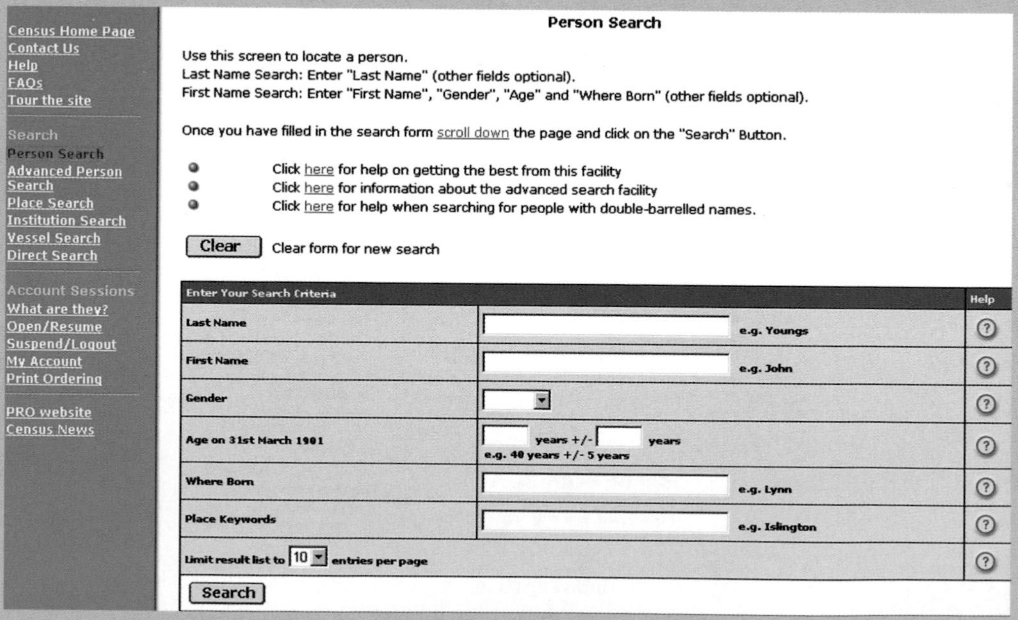

Fig 27 – Search over 32 million individuals on the 1901 Census for England and Wales Web site – **www.census.pro.gov.uk**

The census records are very useful to family history researchers because they document the names and occupations of household occupants, and exact ages and birthplaces in later records. The 1901 Census for England and Wales is now available on the Web at www.census.pro.gov.uk (see Fig 27), allowing you to search over 32 million individuals for free, and download digital images of original census pages for 75p. You pay by credit card or if you do not have a credit card or do not wish to use it, you can buy vouchers. 'Scotland's People' at www.scotlandspeople.gov.uk is also a pay-per-view Web site and census information is available on the Web site of the Public Record Office of Northern Ireland at www.proni.nics.gov.uk

The Internet can also be used to study military records. The Commonwealth War Graves Commission site at www.cwgc.org provides personal details (such as the name of the spouse and parents), service details and places of commemoration for those who died whilst serving with Commonwealth forces during the First and Second World Wars. Web sites like www.forcesreunited.org.uk and www.comradesandcolleagues.com can also be valuable in helping trace old friends of people who used to, or currently, serve with the Forces.

Another line of useful research might be immigration and emigration records. The Internet can help here as well by providing direct access to the national archives of many countries, ship passenger lists and even transportation registers if your ancestor happened to have been sentenced to transportation as a convicted criminal.

Five other steps

1 Find a family tree software program

There are many software programs on the market to help you systematically organise the information you collect about your ancestors. Many of them advertise on the Web or provide free downloads, and you can also compare reviews or get recommendations from current users via message boards.

2 Communicate with other family history researchers

The BBC has a dedicated section on its Web site called 'Your History' at www.bbc.co.uk/history/your_history, which includes a message board called 'Family Trees'.

Subscribing to a mailing list will also allow you to meet like-minded researchers to increase and share your knowledge on the topic or geographical area you are interested in. A Web site called 'Rootsweb' at http://lists.rootsweb.com hosts thousands of mailing lists. Another useful Web site called 'Genuki' lists the relevant mailing list(s) for any county in the UK at www.genuki.org.uk/indexes/MailingLists.html

3 | Contact your local family history society

Local societies often hold lectures, organise visits and provide advice. The Federation of Family History Societies represents over 220 family history societies and genealogical organisations worldwide, although societies in Scotland have their own separate Association, the Scottish Association of Family History Societies. You can look up the contact details, including email address and Web address if available, for a society in your area on their Web sites at www.ffhs.org.uk and www.safhs.org.uk

4 | Search engines

Search engines should not be ignored as tools which can help you trace your family history. Many people get started by simply typing their surname into a search engine.

5 | Research local history

Many local authority Web sites contain information about local places of interest and details of local history clubs and classes.

A Web site called 'Old Maps' at www.old-maps.co.uk provides access to digital historical maps using part of an address, a postcode or a place name.

The BBC Web site called 'Your History' at www.bbc.co.uk/history/your_history also provides useful ideas on how to research a home or town, and includes information about projects and research underway in selected areas.

Chapter 9

Where can I find out more about the Internet?

Just as you need to jump into the driving seat of a car to learn about driving, so you need to take the plunge and start 'surfing' to learn more about the Internet. Follow some of the processes described in this book, and then experiment for yourself.

The Internet is also a resource in itself. You will find many Web sites, newsgroups and mailing lists for internet newcomers providing tips and practical advice. Here are a few ideas for some places to start.

Internet resources

www.bbc.co.uk/webwise

This Web site is a very useful resource, catering for all levels of internet experience. The site includes a step-by-step tutorial, access to instant answers to your questions and articles about topical internet issues.

www.yahoo!.co.uk

Follow the links from the Yahoo Web directory to 'Computers and Internet', followed by 'Internet' and then 'Beginner's Guides' for useful links to beginner's chat sites, guides and internet dictionaries.

Courses

There are also courses available which will help you build confidence and practical experience of the Internet.

Age Concern

Age Concern offers computer taster sessions at around 100 locations across the UK, giving people the chance to use the Internet and learn other computer skills in a friendly and informal environment with other beginners. To find out if there is an Age Concern taster session in your area, look at the Web site (www.ageconcern.org.uk/ITforall) or telephone 020 8765 7610.

UK online centres

New centres offering access to the Internet are opening throughout the UK almost every week. Your nearest centre could be in your local school, your public library, a church or community centre or the offices of a local company. Some will even have staff on hand to show you how to make the most of the Internet. To find out where your nearest centre is call 0800 77 1234.

www.learndirect.co.uk

Learndirect is a government-backed service which provides access to courses available via the Internet, or in one of the national network of Learndirect centres, and can help find the best course for you. Course details can be found on its Web site (www.learndirect.co.uk) or by calling its telephone information line on 0800 100 900.

Further education colleges

Many further education colleges also run internet beginner's classes as well as more advanced courses on subjects such as how to design your own Web site.

Other resources

Magazines such as *Internet Made Easy* and *ComputerActive* are available in newsagents and bookshops or by subscription, and are written in plain English for readers who are new to computers as well as the Internet.

Last but not least, talking to people around you – friends and family – will give you a valuable insight into things that have worked well, or not so well for them, providing a wonderful pool of experience and ideas to dip into.

What will I find on the Internet of interest to me?

You can find anything and everything on the Internet – the only limits are your imagination.

More and more people and companies are realising that creating a Web site is an effective way of publicising their work or sharing their ideas with the rest of the world. This appendix is intended to provide a sample of what is on offer.

1 Holidays and travel

Whether you are planning a short break or a long trip abroad, the Internet can save you a lot of leg-work in comparing prices, checking timetables and planning itineraries.

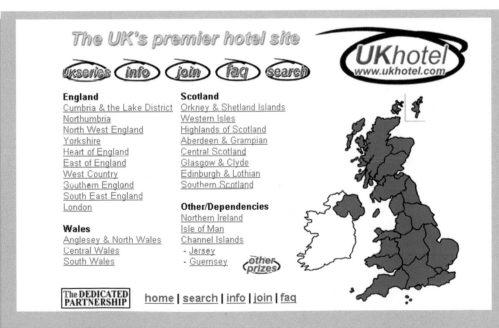

Fig 28 – www.ukhotel.com – Book a hotel anywhere in the UK anytime

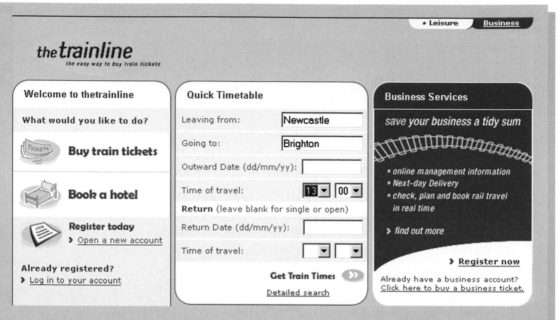

Fig 29 – **www.thetrainline.com** – Plan a train journey using this helpful timetable, check availability and pricing and book tickets

Fig 30 – **www.rac.co.uk** – Plan your car journey before you set out, and avoid the traffic jams

Fig 31 – **www.nationalexpress.com** – Plan your journey by coach and book tickets online

Others like these:

www.cheapflights.co.uk – Compare prices for flights

www.seaview.co.uk – Plan a ferry trip or cruise

www.lonelyplanet.co.uk – An online guidebook to hundreds of travel destinations

www.maps.com – Locate your holiday destination on the map and read articles and reviews about your destination

2 News and sport

You will find equivalents to all your favourite newspapers, television channels and magazines on the Web, providing up to the minute news stories and features.

Fig 32 – www.guardian.co.uk – Guardian newspaper

Fig 33 – **www.sportinglife.com** – Latest British sports news, results, betting prices, statistics and online betting

Others like these:

ww.timesonline.co.uk – *Times* newspaper

www.bbc.co.uk – BBC

www.dailymail.co.uk – Associated New Media

www.racingpost.co.uk – Racing news

www.sky.co.uk – Latest sports news from Sky Sports or the latest news stories from Sky News

3 Arts and entertainment

Find out about the latest shows and art exhibitions and beat the queues to book your ticket.

Fig 34 – www.lastminute.com/theatrenow – Buy discounted tickets for shows at London theatres, or read a round-up of critical reviews

Fig 35 – www.ticketmaster.co.uk – Buy tickets to sport events, concerts, exhibitions, dance performances, etc

(© The National Gallery, London)

Fig 36 – www.nationalgallery.org.uk – Go on a virtual tour of the paintings at the National Gallery

Others like these:

www.royalopera.org.uk – Book your seat at the Royal Opera House

www.somerset-house.org.uk – View the collections of Somerset House

4 Hobbies

Whatever your hobby, you will find Web sites to match your interests and put you in touch with other people who share your passion.

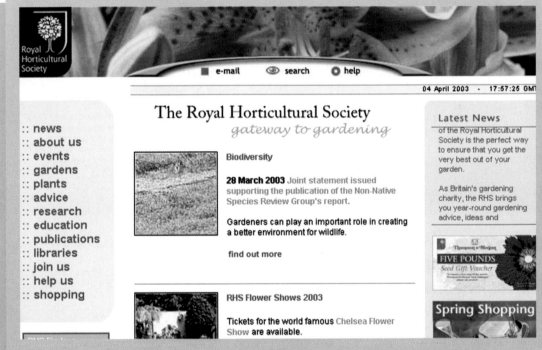

Fig 37 – www.rhs.org.uk – Web site of the Royal Horticultural Society; full of useful plant and garden advice and a very useful checklist of jobs you need to be doing in the garden each month

The Monthly Web Magazine for Birdwatchers   **February 2003**

Home • Bird Guide • Features • News • Reserves • Clubs • Mystery Bird • Gallery • Accommodation • FAQ's • Bird Shop • Tours

Welcome to the Birds Of Britain website. With over 250 pages including changing monthly features and a permanent guide to Britain's bird reserves and clubs, we hope you will find something of interest.

Readers Gallery
Left - Robin photographed by Andy Pilko©. We have lots of new photographs this moth in our Readers Gallery.

This months Feature
Local Nature Reserves
Steve Portugal discusses the importance of Local Nature Reserves to both wildlife and people..

Chris Mead
Sadly, Chris Mead, leading figure in the BTO, died last month. See news page for further details and the BTO's plans to celebrate the life of this dedicated bird champion.

Birding Tours - New Section

IBIS Excursions

■ **Bird Guide**

Illustrated guide to over 100 bird species, with articles written by Michael Seago and others.

■ **Mystery Bird Quiz**

In collaboration with *British Birds* magazine, we are pleased to present a monthly quiz. Some will be relatively easy, others decidedly tricky - so have a

Fig 38 – www.birdsofbritain.co.uk – An invaluable guide for birdwatchers

braingamez.com
intelligent online games

Kenny Cook Atlanta Real Estate Online.

flipside.getminted.com ☒
Hi-Lo
QuickFire Lotto   Play
Slots
Arcade Horses

• **Add to favorites**
• Set as homepage

Get your link here: Join Txtswap for free!

InterWebWord
free multiplayer word game

HangMan

BrainGamez.com Home
Click here to add this page to your Favourites

O N L I N E   G A M E Z :

InterWebWord

Click here to play InterWebWord, an online word game with **real people.**

Click here to play HangMan, an online version of that classic word game.

Fig 39 – www.braingamez.com – Mind-teasers such as hangman and tic-tac-toe to while away a few hours

Antiques World Antiques World - the UK directory of information on antiques and collectables for private and professional enthusiasts.

Events
Major fairs
Local fairs
Exhibitions
Tours
Courses

Organisations
Clubs
Trade
Restoration
Research

Publications
Books
Magazines

Editorial
Articles
Book reviews

Contact us
Email.
(Sorry, but we do not identify or value items, give guidance

Best internet guide to UK fairs and markets

▸ Major national and regional antiques and collectables fairs for the whole of 2003

▸ Hundreds of local antiques and collectables fairs and markets for the next few weeks

Specialist books and price guides

Books available from leading specialist publishers of reference and price guides to antiques and collectables.
Includes Shire, Richard Dennis, Charlton Press.

 Out now>>>>
Wade Decorative Ware Vol2 (3rd edition) - definitive up to date price guide from Charlton Press.

Antiques Trails in UK and Europe by the leading specialist

Tours to leading antiques fairs and markets in the UK and Europe in the company of other antiques enthusiasts.

Study Courses to improve your knowledge and skill

Want to study antiques? Or learn about antique restoration?
Directory of courses

 Antiques Diary - the UK's leading calendar of antiques fairs and markets

Bigger and better than ever.
Thousands of antiques fairs, markets and auctions.
Every other month.
Details and on-line subscription form.

The most comprehensive list of collectors clubs and societies on the Web

Listing around 200 collectors clubs.

Fig 40 – www.antiquesworld.co.uk – UK directory of information on clubs, fairs, exhibitions, books, tours, etc for antiques and collectables

Others like these:

www.playbridge.com – Improve your bridge game

www.ramblers.org.uk – Information about walking in Britain and the Ramblers' Association and its activities

www.diy.co.uk – Full of tips and advice for all your DIY needs

5 Services

The *World* Wide Web is actually also a fantastic way to find out about what is happening, or what is available, in your *local* area.

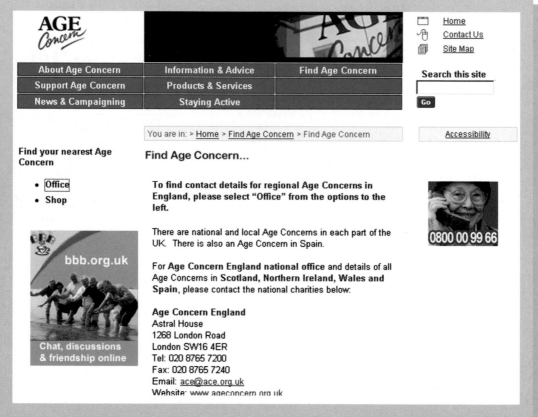

Fig 41 – www.ageconcern.org.uk – Full of useful national and local information for people planning their retirement time

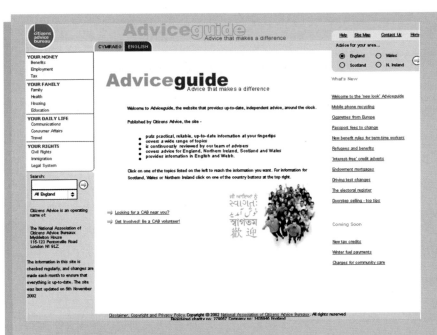

Fig 42 – **www.adviceguide.org.uk** – Provides up-to-date, independent advice, around the clock, on issues such as benefits, tax, housing, travel, etc

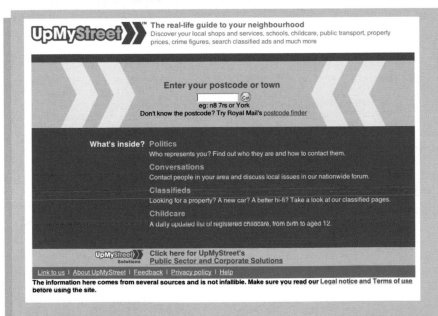

Fig 43 – **www.upmystreet.co.uk** – Look up some interesting facts about where you live, including property prices, Council Tax rates, crime clear-up rates and ambulance response times, or contact people in your area and discuss local issues

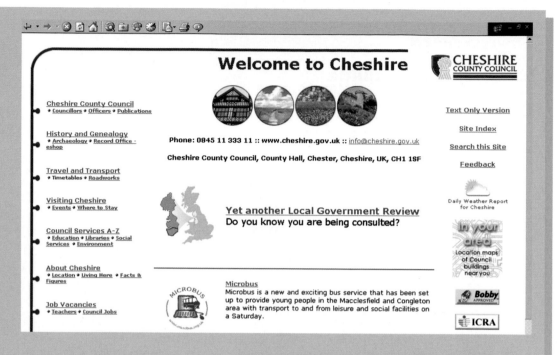

Fig 44 – www.cheshire.gov.uk – Most local authorities have a Web site where you can look up local learning opportunities, leisure facilities, social service information, etc

Others like these:

www.scoot.co.uk – Find whatever local business or service you need

www.bbc.co.uk/voices – A Web site which aims to get to the heart of every community

www.nhs.uk/localnhsservices – Find a dental practice, GP surgery, optician or walk-in NHS centre in your area

6 | Health

Use the Internet to research a health issue or share experiences with others.

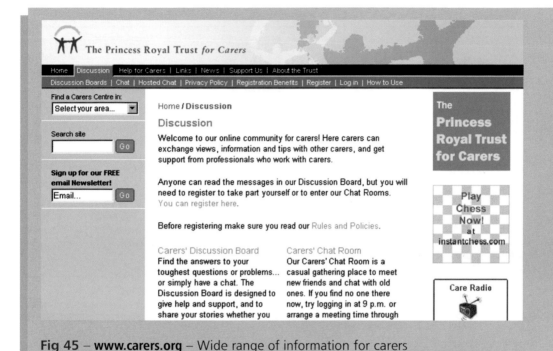

Fig 45 – **www.carers.org** – Wide range of information for carers

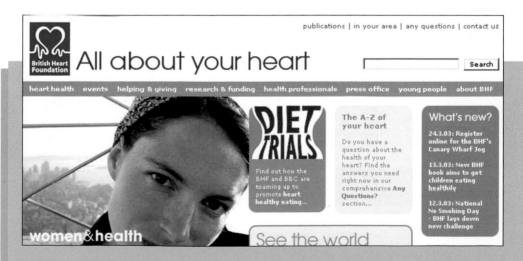

Fig 46 – **www.bhf.org.uk** – Web site of the British Heart Foundation

Fig 47 – **www.netdoctor.co.uk** – Walk into a 'virtual' doctor's surgery

Fig 48 – **www.foodfitness.org.uk** – Discover whether you are an 'activater' or a 'dolittle'

Others like these:

www.depression.org.uk – Resources about stress, anxiety and depression

www.ivillage.co.uk/health – Information and advice on all aspects of women's health and well-being, including complementary therapies

www.diabetes.org.uk – Advice on managing diabetes

About Age Concern

This book is one of a wide range of publications produced by Age Concern England, the National Council on Ageing. Age Concern works on behalf of all older people and believes later life should be fulfilling and enjoyable. For too many this is impossible. As the leading charitable movement in the UK concerned with ageing and older people, Age Concern finds effective ways to change that situation.

Where possible, we enable older people to solve problems themselves, providing as much or as little support as they need. A network of local Age Concerns, supported by many thousands of volunteers, provides community-based services such as lunch clubs, day centres and home visiting.

Nationally, we take a lead role in campaigning, parliamentary work, policy analysis, research, specialist information and advice provision, and publishing. Innovative programmes promote healthier lifestyles and provide older people with opportunities to give the experience of a lifetime back to their communities.

Age Concern is dependent on donations, covenants and legacies.

Age Concern England
1268 London Road
London SW16 4ER
Tel: 020 8765 7200
Fax: 020 8765 7211
Web site:
www.ageconcern.org.uk

Age Concern Scotland
113 Rose Street
Edinburgh EH2 3DT
Tel: 0131 220 3345
Fax: 0131 220 2779
Web site:
www.ageconcernscotland.org.uk

Age Concern Cymru
4th Floor
1 Cathedral Road
Cardiff CF1 9SD
Tel: 029 2037 1566
Fax: 029 2039 9562
Web site:
www.accymru.org.uk

Age Concern Northern Ireland
3 Lower Crescent
Belfast BT7 1NR
Tel: 028 9024 5729
Fax: 028 9023 5497
Web site:
www.ageconcernni.org

Getting the Most from your Computer

Jackie Sherman

This book ranges from the basics of buying and setting up a system, through an introduction to all the commonly-used packages such as *Word*, *Excel* and *PowerPoint*, to more advanced topics so that readers can learn how to create a Web site, produce animated presentations, run their own budget on a spreadsheet or use the desktop publishing features of a word processing package.

£5.99   0-86242-346-5

If you would like to order this or other titles, please write to the address below, enclosing a cheque or money order for the appropriate amount (plus £1.95 p&p) made payable to Age Concern England. Credit card orders may be made on 0870 44 22 044 (for individuals/members of the public); 0870 44 22 120 (AC federation, other organisations and institutions). Fax: 01626 323318. Books can also be ordered online at www.ageconcern.org.uk/shop

Age Concern Books
PO Box 232
Newton Abbot
Devon TQ12 4XQ

Age Concern Information Line/Factsheets subscription

Age Concern produces more than 45 comprehensive factsheets designed to answer many of the questions older people (or those advising them) may have. These include money and benefits, health, community care, leisure and education, and housing. For up to five free factsheets, telephone: 0800 00 99 66 (7am–7pm, seven days a week, every day of the year). Alternatively you may prefer to write to Age Concern, FREEPOST (SWB 30375, ASHBURTON, Devon TQ13 7ZZ.

For professionals working with older people, the factsheets are available on an annual subscription service, which includes updates throughout the year. For further details and costs of the subscription, please write to Age Concern at the above Freepost address.

Glossary

Broadband High-speed internet access with a permanent connection to the Internet, known as 'always on', permitting unlimited use for a fixed monthly charge.

Bulletin board (see Message board)

Cache Web browsers hold copies of recently visited Web pages in a directory on your hard disk. This disk memory space is called the cache. When you return to a page you've recently looked at, the browser can get it from the cache rather than the original server, saving you time. The disadvantage is that it will sometimes show you an old version of a page from your disk when a newer one is available on the Web but you can check for a newer version by using the Refresh or Reload option in your browser.

Chat site A special kind of Web site which enables conversation between people visiting the Web site at the same time. Chat sites are popular as meeting places for people who may never actually meet each other in person, but who can chat to each other like old friends by typing, reading and responding to text messages.

Downloading This is the process of transferring files from a computer on the Internet to your own computer down the telephone line.

E-commerce The process of buying and selling over the Internet.

Email Short for 'electronic mail'. It is the internet version of the postal service. Instead of putting a letter into a postbox, you send a message from your computer down a telephone line to another person who also has access to email.

Email address To exchange email messages with friends and family, and to register for many types of internet services, you need your own email address, which will typically look something like this: **heatherbloggs@hotmail.com**

Hard disk The disk inside your computer where your programs are stored. Disk capacity is measured in megabytes (Mb), or gigabytes (Gb) (a gigabyte is 1,000 megabytes).

Hyperlink A hyperlink may be a word or a graphic. When it is clicked with a mouse, a new Web page, or part of the same page, opens automatically in your Web browser. When a hyperlink is text, it is typically displayed in a different colour and may also be underlined. A text hyperlink that has already been visited is usually displayed in a different colour.

Internet A worldwide collection of computers joined by networks which are linked to each other via communication links such as telephone lines. To join the Internet all you have to do is connect your computer to this network.

Internet Service Provider (ISP) A company which provides you with access to the Internet from your computer.

Mailing list A service that collects messages and broadcasts them to a specific group of people by email, enabling a discussion to take place. Mailing lists usually serve a particular interest group.

Mail server A computer managed by your ISP which gives access to email messages.

Message board A page in a Web site which is used to display a topic or a question to which anyone can respond, and these responses are then displayed for all to read and respond to.

Modem A device which converts the digital data from your computer into sound signals which are transmitted over a standard telephone line, and converts sound signals back again into digital data which can be understood by your computer.

Net (see World Wide Web (WWW))

Network Computers which are joined together by cables and software are called networks. They can swap information and messages between themselves.

Newsgroup An Internet discussion group about a particular topic.

News server A large computer that can store thousands of newsgroups and allow messages to be passed backwards and forwards, enabling anyone to read the content online and to add their own comments.

Offline This means working on a computer that does *not* currently have a 'live' connection to the Internet.

Online This means working on a computer that does currently have a 'live' connection to the Internet.

Operating system This is the software which manages the software applications running on your computer, by performing tasks such as scheduling tasks and use of internal memory between applications running at the same time. All computer equipment and software require an operating system which is why it is usually pre-installed on new computers. A popular operating system for PCs is called *Microsoft Windows*.

POP3 (Post Office Protocol 3) This is the most recent version of a standard for receiving email. It is built into the most popular email programs and Web browsers.

Processor The 'brains' of your computer. The faster the processor's speed (measured in MegaHertz – MHz), the more calculations and data the computer can process.

RAM (Random Access Memory) The memory your computer uses to open and run all the different programs, measured in Megabytes (Mb).

Search engine/directory A special kind of Web site which allows you to enter words or select from a list of subjects and categories to search for a topic. A search engine combs the Web for pages relevant to your search. A Web directory uses real people to add new Web pages to their lists.

Software A computer program or application. Examples are games, accounting and word processing.

URL (Universal Resource Locator) (see Web address)

Web (see World Wide Web (WWW))

Web address Typically looks something like this: http://www.ageconcern.org.uk It identifies the location on the Internet of a Web site or page.

Web browser A type of software that enables your computer to load and display pages in a Web site. The most popular Web browsers are Microsoft's *Internet Explorer* and Netscape's *Navigator*.

Web site A collection of pages which can consist of text, pictures, moving images and sound which together describe an organisation/product/service, etc.

World Wide Web (WWW) Provides a way of viewing the information stored on computers connected to the Internet.